Toward a Christian Marriage

A CHALCEDON STUDY

ELIZABETH FELLERSEN, *Editor*

Ross House Books
P.O. Box 67
Vallecito, CA 95251

First Printed 1972
Second Edition 1994

Library of Congress Catalogue 94-066922
ISBN 1-879998-04-1

In memory of Mark William Fellersen

AUTHORS

Rousas J. Rushdoony, B.A., M.A., University of California, B.D., Pacific School of Religion, is an ordained minister, scholar, writer, and lecturer. A contributor to many theological and philosophical journals, he is the author of the following books and several others forthcoming from Presbyterian and Reformed Publishing Company: *By What Standard?, Intellectual Schizophrenia, Freud, Van Til, This Independent Republic, The Nature of the American System, The Messianic Character of American Education, Bread Upon the Waters, The Biblical Philosophy of History, The Mythology of Science, Foundations of Social Order,* and *The Myth of Over-Population.*

Lawrence R. Eyres, B.A., Wheaton College, Th.B., Westminster Theological Seminary, is an ordained minister and has served congregations in Deerfield, New Hampshire, Westchester, Illinois, Portland, Oregon, and Long Beach, California, two of which he organized. He is now pastor of Redeemer Orthodox Presbyterian Church, Dayton, Ohio. He is the author of numerous articles in *The Presbyterian Guardian.* The Rev. Mr. Eyres has been moderator of the various Presbyteries in which he has served and was moderator of the General Assembly of the Orthodox Presbyterian Church in 1951.

Joel H. Nederhood, A.B., Calvin College, Th.M., Calvin Seminary, Th.D., Free University of Amsterdam, has for more than ten years served in the radio ministry of the Christian Reformed Church. He is now radio minister of the denomination and principal speaker on The Back to God Hour radio broadcast. Dr. Nederhood is the author of: *God is Too Much* (Tyndale House Publishers) and *The Holy Triangle* (Baker Book House).

INTRODUCTION

When this book was first printed some years ago, it sold quickly and well, and it was generally well received. There was, however, a surprisingly negative response from a number of women, especially to my chapter. By letter, in a few printed statements, and to me in person during my travels, more than a few women saw my position as morally wrong and as definitely "sub-Christian."

The disagreement was not exegetical. I was not told that I had wrongly read and interpreted Scripture. Rather, the common reaction was that my position did not reflect "New Testament Christianity" and was "unspiritual."

These readers were not modernists. They were fundamentalists and ostensible reformed believers. Dispensationalism for the first group meant that my position was obviously "legalistic." The supposedly reformed women lacked the extreme dispensationalism of the others, but they did have two dispensations, the Old and the New Testament eras. We are now, it is held, in a new era and no longer under law. Therefore, the various spheres of life are now governed "spiritually," not by the law. This position assumes that the Holy Spirit who with the Father and the Son gave the law no longer requires obedience to it. Not surprisingly, immoralism is a major problem in the church.

The law, God's way of holiness or sanctification, is not preached in most churches. What is preached instead is a vague, antinomian spirituality. The focus is humanistic. It is on what God can do for you if you follow spiritual concerns. The faith is not related to the problems of the world, nor to the Kingdom of God, but to finding inner peace by spiritual thinking and living. What is meant by this strongly resembles the concerns of the late medieval pietism. Let the world fall apart while you seek a peace of heart and mind.

Such an emphasis is hostile to both the Bible and the Reformation. It is a flight from, not an overcoming of, the world. There are implicit Manichaean elements to such thinking.

Also, the critics were feminists within the church, "spiritual" rather than militant feminists.

The church has concentrated on John 3:16 in isolation from the Kingdom of God. Its "spiritual" preaching is very low in theology. Unlike the early church, there is no systematic preaching, verse by verse, on one book of the Bible after another. Biblical history and law are neglected, and this perverts preaching into a vague neo-platonic spirituality.

As a result, too many church members get their world and life view from the world, not from God, because churches see the Bible as a spiritual manual, not as God's marching orders for all of life and for all men.

It is embarrassing to ask, and I no longer do so, when faithful church members last heard a sermon on any of the Ten Commandments. It is equally bad to ask anyone to name the Ten Commandments. If the church is so stripped of the law of God, is it any wonder that our society is?

Sadly, the situation is no better in other churches. The Rev. John C. Miller, Catholic priest and editor of the *Social Justice Review*, wrote, in the January-February 1994 issue that "Morally speaking, homosexual actions are wrong because they are contrary to nature." This argument has been invalid since at least the time of the Marquis de Sade. Sade recognized the fallen and depraved nature of man and nature. He saw that Christian morality goes *against* our fallen nature rather than expressing it. He saw Christianity and its law as unnatural.

Because we are a fallen people living in a fallen world order, Christianity requires us to work to establish a regenerate life and order. As we are converted, we must convert all things, bringing every sphere of life and thought into captivity to Christ.

The key sphere, and our starting point, is the family. As regenerate men and women, we must establish Godly families. God's law tells us that civil government shall receive only a small tax in order to "atone," cover, or protect us (Ex. 30:11-16). In Numbers 18:25-26, we see that the tithe to the Lord was given to the Levites, who then gave a tithe of the tithe to the priests for the sanctuary. In other words, God limited the income of both state and church because He did not want either to become the dominant institution.

This meant that the strong institution in terms of God's law-word is neither church nor state but the family. A truly Godly order requires that the family have priority.

This does not mean that the family is sinless or flawless; any married man or woman knows otherwise. It does mean that the family has a centrality in the Christian life and the Kingdom of God. Apart from a truly Godly family, no church nor state can be strong.

How important the family is to civilization was developed by Carle C. Zimmerman in *Family and Civilization* (1947) and by Lucius F. Cervantes in *Marriage and the Family* (1956). These exceptionally important works received very little attention from the university and the churches. The non-Christian public also turned to a vast number of books whose emphasis was purely physical, such as Jodi Lawrence's *The Search for the Perfect Orgasm* (1973). The emphasis in this century has shifted from marriage and the family to sexual experience, with obviously sorry results. Lawrence's goal is the "humanistic orgasm" as "the ultimate," not the family.

The churches, having abandoned God's law, increasingly take their standards from the world. An appalling fact is that decision of various church bodies to appoint committees to study and report on abortion, homosexuality, and other matters, as though God had not already provided a sufficient report called the *Bible*!

Now marriage is for time only. Our Lord makes clear that in the resurrection there is neither marriage nor giving in marriage (Luke 20:35). And yet the law of God makes clear how important and how central marriage is. God the Son came into the world neither through church nor state but into a family. This tells us that marriage, although non-existent in heaven is all the same central to this world. We are to live here as physical creatures under God whose lives are given their great training ground in terms of the Kingdom of God by marriage. Our Lord stresses the fact that marriage is our normal calling (Matt. 19:10-12).

A great emphasis of the Reformation was on the Godliness of Christian marriage. There was exuberant preaching in England, for example, on Genesis 26:8, "behold, Isaac was sporting with Rebekah his wife." They were insistent that both the joys and duties of life are marital. The revival of a strong patriarchal family life was a major source of Protestant vitality.

Zimmerman and Cervantes, in *Marriage and the Family* wrote,

> From birth to grave, there is scarcely any great action of consequence that can be performed by a person, even in our free society, that is not guided and colored by family relations. The individual in his family

> meaning is the real unit in society. Detached or nonfamilistically guided individuals exist only in imagination or in discolored surroundings such as prostitution, crime, or skid row. (p.31)

This is an obvious fact, and yet too little is said from the pulpit about the importance of Christian marriage.

The family is the great transmitter of faith and culture. Where the family weakens or fails, we have a return to barbarism, a fact very evident in our time. There can be no effectual social reconstruction apart from the Christian family. Any institution or group that does not strengthen the family is contributiong to the downfall of civilization. God ordained marriage for the welfare and happiness of mankind. To neglect marriage and the family for neoplatonic spirituality is both wrong and sinful.

Evolutionary thinking has been anti-familistic and has contributed to our current moral crisis. The family is more than a biological fact; it is not merely an evolutionary stage. It is God's purpose for mankind; it is a blessing. Certainly, the fall has commonly vitiated and hindered that blessing, but, in a true Christian marriage, that blessing is a marvellous and holy fact.

Rousas John Rushdoony
Vallecito, California
February 15, 1994

CONTENTS

Rousas J. Rushdoony

THE DOCTRINE OF MAN

Genesis 2

We have seen in our studies of the first chapter of Genesis that there is a great line of cleavage between Biblical thought and all other thinking. Every philosophy or religion which assumes, *as all others do*, that man evolved out of a primeval chaos then posits that the ultimate power in its system of thought is primeval chaos. But we as Christians, because we believe God created all things by His Word, believe that the source of our power is not below but above—in God.

Thus, whenever society needs renewal, whenever man needs regeneration, the source of regeneration for *us* is in God. Because their source, their origin, is in chaos, when the adherents of every other philosophy and religion want social renewal, the answer for *them* is chaos or revolution. Hence, every non-Christian religion and philosophy is in varying degree a religion of revolution, a chaos cult; it requires, it calls for revolution—chaos—in order to revive society. So, whenever things begin to deteriorate, *their* answer is to invoke chaos, revolution. *Our* answer is to establish things again under the law of God because *we* look to *God* for our renewal; *they*, to *chaos*.

The doctrine of man is very closely related to this whole background. If men hold, as all non-Christian systems do, that man is a product of evolution, evolution arising out of the primeval chaos, then the thing that is least important in man is *reason*. Why? Well, according to them, reason evolved last of all. Therefore, to understand man you do not look to reason. You look to man's emotions. To understand man, according to modern psychiatry and sociology and according to every kind of modern thought, you look progressively downward. You look not to the mature, thinking man to understand man; but you look to the child and to child psychology and say, "This will help us to understand man." But you do not stop there. You look then to primitive man because "Primitive man is even more basic than the child; he is closer to primeval chaos." But you do not stop there, either. You go further backward to animals; and you look behind animals to primeval chaos; and thereby you understand man. Hence it is, for example, in Freudian psychology that reason is nothing; and the basic primitive impulses in man, which are traced downward progressively, are all-important. This is what Cornelius Van Til, the philosopher of religion, has called "integration into the void." To understand man in these systems, you have an integration into the void, integration downward.

If you believe that man was created in the image of God, then you understand man not in terms of the child or primitive man or animals or, ultimately, chaos; but you understand him in terms of the image of God: *knowledge, righteousness, holiness,* and *dominion.* The standard for man then is the *mature* man, the perfect man; and man is not struggling out of a primeval background, but he is in rebellion against maturity. A Christian psychology would look at things not as the Freudian does, not as all non-Christian psychologies do, by an integration downward, but by an insistence that man instead of being a bundle of primitive urges is a sinner who is rebelling against maturity; that he was created into this maturity; that the Fall of man was a rebellion against maturity, and the whole of man's being today, when he is outside of Christ, is a headlong flight and rebellion against the requirement of maturity.

The modern conception of man is one of total irresponsibility. Henry Miller has said in one of his most expressive sentences, "I think it's bad to think."[1] Why? Because reason is a latecomer. He says the way to restore paradise is to give vent to every desire, every appetite you have—and the more primitive these expressions are, the more powerful they will be, and the sooner they will restore paradise. The modern conception of man, therefore, is one of integration downward into total irresponsibility.

The Biblical conception is submission through the grace of God in Jesus Christ to the law of God.

It is interesting to see how irresponsibility is the standard for men

1. George Wickes, "Henry Miller at Seventy," an interview in *Claremont Quarterly*, vol. 9, no. 2 (Winter, 1962), p. 9.

today by looking at movies and TV. The TV and movie male hero, I think, is best expressed—most popularly expressed if we are to believe the commentators—in the cowboy hero. Having lived in the inter-mountain area in Nevada and having served as a pastor there and having seen some of Idaho and Colorado, it is very revealing to me that the cowboy should be the hero because the cowboy is the most immature and irresponsible man in our society.

The sheepherder is not a hero; in fact, in the inter-mountain country the sheepherder is despised and looked down upon; but the sheepherder is a responsible person, and it is not common for a sheepherder to die poor. It is next to impossible to get an American today to be a sheepherder. The only way they can get sheepherders nowadays is to import them; a few come from Mexico, but most of them under a special immigration quota come from the south of France and the north of Spain—the Basques—and from Greece. They come over here in their late teens. They make a fair amount of money, two or three hundred dollars a month—sometimes a little more; with all their food provided and a sheepwagon to live in, this is almost all potentially savings. When they have been here five to ten years, they have saved up quite a few thousand dollars to go into business or to buy their own sheep ranch; and we have to import another sheepherder. They live alone with the sheep; they have to act as midwife when the ewes give birth to their lambs; they have to be ready at any time of night or day if bears or coyotes come around; they do their own cooking; when time hangs heavy on their hands, they knit or read. They are very responsible, self-sufficient people.

Not so the cowboy. The only cowboy in modern history to end up with any money was Death Valley Scotty; and somebody used him as a front —he did not make it. The average cowboy is a drifter and a no-account; he lives just for today. He makes as much as the sheepherder; but he goes into town—and I have given many of them a lift into town and a lift home afterwards—and blows all his pay for three or six months, as the case may be. I have had more than one of them tell me that he went into town with $2,000, and after the first evening he could not remember what he did or where he went; all he knew was he was now broke and hungry and had to get back to the ranch. Very often he was so hungry after having been on a long binge that I had to give him a hamburger to tide him over. Totally irresponsible.

This is the modern standard—and fittingly so—because modern man, dominated as he is by anti-Christian thinking, by evolutionary thinking, by this concept of integration downward into the void, sees as his standard this concept of total irresponsibility, which the cowboy represents. So many cowboys I knew—or, buckaroos, as they were called—were 65 and beginning to fail; yet beyond the clothes on their backs they did not have a thing. It is ironic that in our society today and in our TV and movies these men are exalted, and the glorification of brute strength—the caveman type of thing—is so commonplace. Yet there was never a time in history when brute physical strength was less needed, when size was less an asset; now more than ever unskilled labor is disappearing. Yet we are increasingly emphasizing *irresponsibility* as the ideal for men when men must, more than ever before, be *responsible*. Unhappily, it is having its effect: in schools every year the gap between the boys and the girls widens as the boys do more and more poorly, and the girls get the good grades.

In society at large today, man is the child. He is more given to tantrums, incapable of meeting responsibilities emotionally, given to acting like the child when he should set the pattern for self-control, steadiness, thoughtfulness, and above all, for *worship*.

In churches across country today there is no question that the women predominate. In most homes it is the mother who sees to it that the children get to Sunday school, or they do not get there at all; the responsibility is left to the women. But, according to Scripture, the primary responsibility religiously and morally is the *man's*: the man is, in a very real sense, a priest under God, required to lead in the private religious exercises of the family as well as in the public religious worship of the family.

Man has been created by God in His image, and man having the authority under God in the household is called upon to be *the* principle of authority and of order in society.

It has been very interesting lately to see some of the studies that biologists have turned up which thoroughly militate against their own psychology and against their evolutionary thinking—that is why they are disregarding them. Freud based his theories on man and sex on zoo animals; and many Freudians concluded that 'Sex is the basic factor in animal life; and, therefore, since man is an evolving animal, in the life of man.' But in recent years every study by biologists of animals in their native habitats has shown a very interesting fact: in the whole of the animal world, when animals are free and out in nature, sex is a long way from being the most important thing to the male animal. The two basic drives of animals in nature are status and territoriality—order and property. A male animal in nature will have a territory staked out; a rhinoceros will have every rock, every tree, and every inch of the river staked out that is his territory; and if any other male rhino crosses that—unless he is subordinate and part of his herd—it means a pitched battle; his sense of order and of property is that strong. Birds are the same. Those of you who have ever done any bird watching know that a portion of your yard will belong to a particular bird, and no other bird of that variety dare cross over that area. There is a very strong and a rigid sense of property among all *wild* animals. It is only in *caged* animals that sex becomes important above order and property—because they live in a welfare economy, they don't have to worry about these things.

So it is when man begins to live in a welfare society that he ceases to be the kind of man God created him to be—one who is the source of order in the community and one who has a strong sense of property. Instead, he becomes like a caged animal, living primarily in terms of sex.

Man created in the image of God—knowledge, righteousness, holiness, and dominion—must show forth these things in his everyday life.

He must show forth the *holiness* of God in his being. He cannot, therefore, follow nature. He must follow God and His Word. Hence, everything that naturalism and evolutionary thinking says is basic to man and calls for an integration downward is anathema to him. Essential to his being, of course, is being a material creature; and he must never despise the things of this earth, his body and the world around him; but all these things are subject to *order,* and the order *comes from God.*

Man must be the one who establishes order in his family and in his community. Man cannot, therefore, be the playboy who leaves morality and religion to his wife. If he obeys the Word of God, he must be *the* most moral member of the family. In the Mosaic law—and very few people are aware of this, but it is spelled out there repeatedly—there are 18 death penalties for men and only a few for women. A number of crimes require the death penalty for men but not for women. Why? Because the greater the responsibility, the greater the culpability; and God has given a greater responsibility to *men.* In the Mosaic law, the adultery of a man is a far more serious thing than that of a woman; and God punishes it more grievously because a man as the head of the household, as the source of order in society under God, must establish the pattern of conduct. Thus it is that God declared through the prophets that He would not punish the adultery of their wives and daughters when the fathers and sons themselves were so perverse in their morality. Instead, He said, 'I will bring judgment upon this entire generation and this society' (Hosea 4:14).

Man is called to exercise *dominion.* It means that he has a calling under God to exercise dominion in every area of life: scientific, agricultural, religious, commercial—in every area man is to exercise dominion. It is significant that in Genesis 2 we read that Adam was created and immediately given responsibility: the care of the garden of Eden, an agricultural task. He was required to name the animals, a scientific task. The word 'name' in the Hebrew means 'to classify, to identify'; and in the Bible, names themselves were classifications—a man's name could change a number of times, depending upon his character. So when Adam was called upon to name the animals, it was a work of classification. It perhaps took years. We do not know how long the period was before the Fall—it could have been decades.

Under God, man must, first of all, exercise dominion over *himself;* he must govern himself. If he cannot respect his God-given manhood sufficiently to govern himself, he need not be surprised if others fail to respect him. If he cannot be emotionally mature, how can he expect those under his authority to be so?

It is significant that it was only after a long period, apparently—after Adam had tended the garden of Eden and had named the animals—that God made Eve for him. We are told that Adam saw that there was male and female in all of the world around him ". . . but for Adam there was not found an help meet for him" (Genesis 2:20). Eve was not created immediately; she appears on the scene only after a considerable time: Adam has been created and given the responsibility of the garden of Eden; he has named all the animals, an extensive work of classification. Then and then only is he given Eve. In other words, before marriage, *responsibility*. He first proved himself a *man* in relationship to work, in relationship to his calling; and then under God he was ready for marriage. Marriage came not as a fulfillment of his physical needs but as the consummation of his fulfillment *as a man under God*.

Again, it is significant that in the Mosaic law we find the dowry system as a part of marriage. Normally the dowry system required that the equivalent of three years' wages be supplied by the groom to the bride. This was a considerable sum; he had to work a number of years and save what he earned in order to accumulate the equivalent of three years' wages. He handed it over to the bride-to-be or to her father, who then turned it over to the bride-to-be. This money was not for the wife to spend at her whim; this was the *family's capital*. The husband could use it for business reasons, but he had to give her an allowance for the use of it and he had to repay it. She could not alienate it; it went to the heirs. But, if he should wrong her and, contrary to the law of God, divorce her, then it was her money. If it was justifiable divorce according to the Mosaic law, then the money returned to him. This gave the family a great deal of security because the man did not lightly break up a marriage when his bankroll was tied up in it and because before marriage he had proved his sense of responsibility by accumulating that dowry.

Man must show forth God's image in *knowledge*. He should be, therefore, *the* student above all others of the Word of God. He should be the most knowing, the most capable where wisdom is concerned in the family. There is this difference between wisdom and learning: learning is the accumulation of data; wisdom is the insight to discriminate. A man must exercise knowledge in this sense. Unfortunately, men today are usually the most ignorant of the Word of God, the most unwilling to learn. It is significant that in pornography trials the defense attorneys want men on the juries because they can be sure that the men have not read a book since they left college and they are not going to read the book that is on trial—they will take the word of one or another of the attorneys. The women will take the book into the jury room and sit up nights and read it.

Man was created by God to be *the responsible creature.* Yet today, because men are brought up in an evolutionary faith and taught a religion of revolution, they are *the irresponsible* members of society.

It has amazed me over the years to encounter people in prominent positions who are really very irresponsible. I am thinking of one person in northern California who is one of the most prominent citizens of the area: he is so irresponsible that his wife has to dole him out a little money each day and no more because he is not capable of handling money; she cannot allow him to handle any business because, despite his excellent income, they would be very quickly bankrupt; without her they would be in serious trouble; he is nothing but a facade. This is commonplace.

Men today are dominated by this sense of irresponsibility, by this feeling that they are a *man* if they fulfill the modern TV and movie idea of irresponsibility.

But God created man *in His image,* and He created woman not to be his keeper but as a help meet before him.

One of the greatest needs of our generation today is for *godly men,* responsible men, men who know that they exercise authority, are ready to exercise it under God, and who are the heads of their households and the sources of order and stability in society at large. God give us more such men.

ALMIGHTY GOD, our heavenly Father, we thank Thee that

Thou hast made us, that Thou hast summoned us in Jesus Christ from our irresponsibility and rebellion against maturity and hast given us the responsibility of exercising dominion under Thee. And we pray that by Thy blessing every man here present may grow in grace, in knowledge, in holiness, in righteousness in the exercise of his God-given dominion. In Jesus' name. Amen.

October 3, 1965

Rousas J. Rushdoony

THE DOCTRINE OF MARRIAGE

Genesis 2:15-25

Man was created in the image of God in knowledge, righteousness, holiness, and dominion; and he was created to fulfill his image mandate, his calling under God: to be king over creation, priest therein, and prophet of God. *The Westminster Shorter Catechism* begins by asking

> What is the chief end of man?
> The chief end of man is to glorify God and to enjoy Him forever.

This is man's calling. This is man's destiny.

Adam was not given his help meet, Eve, until some time had elapsed. We are not told in Scripture how long a period this was; it could have been decades between the creation of Adam and the creation of Eve, because Eve was not given to Adam to fulfill a physical need but only when he had proven himself as a responsible person that he might fulfill his destiny under God with her as his help meet. For years Adam labored, classifying all of the animal creation, taking care of the garden, recognizing that throughout nature there was male and female but there was no help meet, no female, for him: first, to prove himself as responsible—this was the requirement; then, marriage. This was reflected in the dowry system of Biblical times, whereby a young man had to labor and accumulate savings equal to three years' wages; then only could he qualify for marriage.

It is interesting that the Hebrew word for a bridegroom is 'the circumcised one'; the Hebrew word for the father-in-law is 'the circumciser' and for mother-in-law, the feminine form of the word circumciser. Certainly, they did not perform the act of circumcision; this was performed on the eighth day after the birth of the man child. To understand the meaning of these names, let us examine the ritual of circumcision.

Circumcision in the Old Testament was comparable to baptism; performed on the eighth day, circumcision signified that this child was now taken into the covenant of grace; he had been born into the fellowship, into the community of the church. It also indicated that the parents believed that in generation there was no hope of salvation, that a person could not be saved by birth, but only by re-generation. The act of circumcision, which involved cutting off the foreskin, in a sense was a way of saying, 'In generation there is no hope; and we have, so to speak, cut off hope in terms of natural regeneration. We believe it must be an act of God.'

Circumcision was a *sign* of membership in the covenant. It meant that the boy had been born into the family of grace, into the covenant. When he reached maturity and had passed the course of studies in the law of God, then he became accepted in the covenant.

Full acceptance, in a sense, came only with marriage. It was the responsibility of every father, before giving his daughter in marriage to any man, to satisfy himself and his wife concerning not only the young man's ability to be a provider: 'Have you worked? Have you accumulated the equivalent of three years' wages so that there be capital for the family?' But also, the faith of the young man: 'What do you believe? Are you going to be under God a prophet, priest, and king? Are you going to fulfill your responsibilities as a *king* (that is, to exercise lordship in the Lord) in your family, in your calling—wherever you are, to be a man under God? Will you be a *priest* unto God, leading your household in religious worship, taking all that you do and dedicating yourself, your family, and your substance unto God? Will you be a *prophet*—that is, will you speak for God? Will you stand for Him so that in your particular calling your standards will be godly and you will show forth righteousness?'

Although the priests and the Levites examined the boy when it came time for confirmation, the real test of his circumcision rested with the father-in-law and the mother-in-law. When they said, 'You may marry our daughter,' he then became 'the circumcised one.' His circumcision was now a reality, spiritually as well as physically; he was truly a man in the covenant. Hence, the name of the bridegroom: 'the circumcised one.'

The Hebrew name for the bride was 'the complete (or, perfected) one. This was her fulfillment; this was her calling: to be a wife, to be a help meet. So, marriage was seen as her completion and her maturity.

Marriage, according to Genesis 2, is a divine ordinance instituted by God. Both work and marriage are institutions in paradise, in the garden of Eden. Those who speak of work as a product of the Fall of man are wrong; his work was cursed after the Fall because he was fallen and everything the fallen man does is under a curse. But when we are redeemed, we move out from under the curse to the blessing of God so that our work, our marriage, our everyday life is no longer under a curse but under blessing.

God's Word concerning man, as at the very beginning He planned for the first marriage, was, "It is not good that the man should be alone." In this single sentence we have the essential meaning of marriage. Many churches say the essential meaning of marriage is procreation—having children; but if this were true, it would mean that a childless marriage is an invalid marriage. Certainly none of these churches is ready to face this conclusion of its position. "It is not good that the man should be alone." God established marriage not for procreation—this is a blessing of marriage—but as fellowship, one life together in terms of man's calling; hence the delay after this Word from God concerning the marriage of Adam (before He gave Eve) so that he might find himself in terms of his manhood: in terms of his responsibility, in terms of his calling under God to be a man—prophet, priest, and king. *Then* the help meet, Eve, was given to him so that he might have fellowship in his calling.

"Therefore shall a man leave . . . and cleave. . . ." With responsibility a man shall leave his father and mother—not before. When he is responsible, then he can be freed, then he can cleave to his wife and create a new unit of society—the family; and the family is *the basic unit of society*.

But the basic unit of society in *our* day is the *individual*. When the individual is the basic unit of society, the individual is very quickly lost in the state.

Very little work has been done in the study of the family. We can be grateful that Dr. Carle C. Zimmerman at Harvard has spent his lifetime studying the history of the family. He has written three volumes; the first and third, I think, are outstanding (his own statist inclinations come out in the second volume). He has pointed out the significance of the family in civilization: that whenever the atomistic family develops, in which the authority of the father is no longer paramount, then there is a very quick disintegration of society, the total state takes over, and there is a radical collapse of civilization. Then out of the ruins here and there a strong family develops until again there is a family-oriented civilization. With the development of the atomistic family—which is really no family at all—the home is simply a place to room and board while the state takes over the role as father—to take care of the family in its every need, providing for the children and the parents; the family no longer cares for itself; civilization collapses.

In the Biblical pattern, the family is the central institution in society:

The family is man's first *church* because it is there that he gets his basic learning concerning the faith.

The family is man's first *school,* for it is in the family that he learns the basic wisdom and learning of all education. It is significant that up to almost a hundred years ago, beginning in the origins of the United States, it was considered unthinkable to send your child to school without first having taught him to read. He went to school not to learn to read but to acquire knowledge in various fields. The colonial mothers would teach their children to read almost as soon as they began to talk—between two and three; thus, when you read of five-year-old boys beginning to study Hebrew in colonial America, you know the reason why.

The family is man's first *state* because the family under God *is* a state. It is there that force is brought to bear on the child to make him conform to what is just: he is punished for evildoing or disobedience; he is taught that there must be law and order within the framework of the family and society at large.

The family as church, as state, and as school is to be headed by the father—prophet, priest, and king under God. This does not mean that he assumes every responsibility or that he takes time to teach the child to read and write or other things. It does mean as *the* person with authority he is responsibile for seeing that these things be done.

Man in the garden of Eden, Adam, learned two things before he married: the pattern of *responsibility* and the pattern of *obedience.* Until Adam served God first, he could not expect the woman to serve him.

Now, in our culture most churches, because of their theology, expect God to serve man. Is it surprising, then, that women expect men to serve them? The whole world is turned upside-down. When you have men expecting God to serve them and women expecting men to serve them, you have social collapse.

The term used in Genesis 2 for Eve is "help meet," a very significant word. "Help meet" is a translation of several Hebrew words which mean 'a help as before him.' We can convey the idea in two ways.

Paul declares in Corinthians that even as man was created in the image of God, so woman was created in the image of man—so that the image of God in woman is a reflected image, a secondhand image, as it were. (Man is created directly in the image of God.)

Moreover, 'a help as before him' means 'a mirror': first, she mirrors *his image;* second, in a sense, she mirrors *him* so that a man finds himself not only in relationship to God but in terms of a woman.

It does make a difference in the character of men when they become married. Insurance statistics bear this out: a young man pays a very high insurance as a driver until he marries; then it drops because he has assumed responsibility, he has become stable, and he has, so to speak, found himself. At least this is true in sufficiently large numbers of cases to make a marked difference in insurance statistics.

The woman is called his "help meet," his mirror; and even as he mirrors God, she mirrors him. He understands his responsibility by looking to God, and he can see how he is fulfilling his responsibilities and proving his obedience in relationship to his wife as she mirrors his nature and responsibility.

Thus, when God felt that Adam had proved himself by his obedience and by his responsibility, He "caused a deep sleep to fall upon Adam, and he slept: and he took one of his ribs (or, 'took from the side of him') . . . and . . . made he a woman, and brought her unto the man. And Adam said, This is now bone of my bones, and flesh of my flesh. . . ." This is a magnificent statement; and part of it is almost untranslatable because the word translated "this is now" is an idiom in the Hebrew which has meaning comparable to what we mean when we say, 'I've got the beat. This is the rhythm of the music, the rhythm of my life that I have been waiting for.' "Bone of my bone" means 'the structure of my life.' The skeleton is the structure of the body, that which supports the body; the body would be like that of a jellyfish without the skeleton. Adam says, "She is bone of my bones" ('The structure of my being is the structure of her being'). "Flesh of my flesh" ('The very life of me is the life of her; I find myself, I realize myself in terms of her').

This brings up a very significant point, one very central to our time. From this, the first marriage, we have a pattern established which is to be the pattern of all marriage: since the woman is to be a help meet to the man in terms of his calling, mixed marriages religiously are from the Biblical perspective wrong. A Christian should not marry an unbeliever or one of another religion because a Christian to fulfill himself in terms of his calling must marry someone who is 'a help as before him,' someone who mirrors that which he is. How can the woman be that mirror and have the community that comes from being the reflected image of the man if her background is so different from that which his is? They must have *a common faith,* or, according to the law of God, it is not a valid marriage.

Moreover, if she is to be 'a help as before him,' a mirror, there must be a common cultural background. This militates against marriages across cultures and across races where there is no common culture or association possible.

The new unit is a continuation of the old unit but an independent one; and there has to be a unity or else it is not a marriage. Thus, the attempt of many today to say there is nothing in the Bible against mixed marriages whether religiously or culturally is altogether unfounded. We do not have to go to the Mosaic law (Exodus and Deuteronomy) to demonstrate that, because here in the very *beginning* (Genesis) we are told that she must be a help meet—bone of his bone, flesh of his flesh—sharing his faith, sharing a common background, a common culture, a common desire to fulfill his calling under God. This, then, is the meaning of marriage in the Biblical sense.

The family (fatherhood) is an important part of the man's calling, but it is not the central part. The family is central to the woman: her responsibility under God is her husband and then the family. Man's responsibility is broader: it is in terms of his work and his total calling under God. The family is a *part* of his responsibility but by no means his total responsibility; his goal is set in terms of his work, which he must view under God. Thus, my wife has observed, "Men live to work, and women work to live."—because their perspective is different.

In all of these things man today is rebelling against God. Woman, on the other hand, because she is created in the image of man—the reflected image of God—does not rebel directly against God. She can go to church and be as pious and sanctimonious as you please because she shows rebellion by her rebellion against her husband, who represents the authority of God as she is to know it. The rebellion of men is directly against God; the rebellion of women, indirectly against God and directly against the authority, the godly authority, of the husband.

"Therefore shall a man leave his father and his mother, and shall cleave unto his wife: and they shall be one flesh." Having assumed the status of a man in marriage, though he continues to honor his father and his mother and has responsibilities toward them, he is now directly under God; and, therefore, he must create an independent entity, a new home. He can no longer have anyone over him in the sense of a family relationship; *he is directly under God as a man.* He must leave father and mother not only by departing from the home and establishing a new home, but he must also cease to be dependent upon them. While retaining, of course, a loving relationship and honoring them, he must cut the apron strings.

He must *leave* father and mother and *cleave* unto his wife because by that leaving and that cleaving he establishes this new entity and asserts, 'I will now be a responsible man under God and will fulfill my mandate to be a prophet, priest, and king under Him.'

In brief, this, then, is the Biblical doctrine of marriage ordained in paradise and instituted together with work as central parts of man's calling.

OUR LORD AND OUR GOD, we thank Thee that Thou hast established and ordained marriage for the welfare and happiness of mankind. We thank Thee that Thou hast called us into Christian marriages, made us husbands and fathers, wives and mothers in Jesus Christ. Bless each home that is here represented that by Thy grace we may grow and mature in terms of our calling, rejoice in one another in Thee and under Thee, and might all the days of our life know the joy and the strength that comes from being heirs together of the grace of life. Bless us to this purpose. In Jesus' name. Amen.

October 10, 1965

Lawrence R. Eyres

THE WORLD'S MOST NOTABLE HOME BUILDERS

Proverbs 14:1

I feel that it is not so much that today is Mother's Day as it is the Lord's Day. Yet, since some feel—for the sake of their mothers—that this is a special day, I feel that I must bring from the Word of God instruction and encouragement; and if perchance there be a word of correction, reproof, or rebuke, I still must bring it from the Word of God.

We think of home builders as contractors who build dream homes which all of us want and none of us can afford, but I am thinking of those who really build *homes*. A home in the sense of the Word of God is the people who dwell together under God's ordinances as a family in the name and authority of Jesus Christ with the love of Christ flowing through everything they do, submitting to one another in His love and His obedience. In this sense women are home builders.

"Every wise woman buildeth her house: but the foolish plucketh it down with her hands." What is *wisdom* in the sense of our text? Proverbs 31:30 tells us, "Favour is deceitful, and beauty is vain: but a woman that feareth the Lord, she shall be praised." Elsewhere in Scripture we read that it is the fear of the Lord that is the beginning of wisdom—and the word 'beginning' means the first part, the middle, and the end (Psalm 111:10; Proverbs 9:10). The pure essence of wisdom is that men and women fear God. The fear of God is, first of all, the worship of God, recognizing that He is the great, the sovereign, and mighty God over us and that we are His creatures made in His image, made to fulfill a function and to reflect glory back to Him in terms of what He has made us and called us in grace to be. Of course, there is a trembling fear in this fear; and that trembling fear is the recognition that this God is a jealous God and does indeed visit the iniquities of the fathers upon the children. He does, indeed, visit iniquity upon those who reject and rebel against His ordinances and do not wish to fulfill the role in life unto which He has called them. Wisdom, in the end, is nothing more than submitting to God and actively going along with God's purposes for us, seeking His mercy and forgiveness for our sins, desiring to be obedient to Him in all things, and honoring Him as God in all the relations of life.

Foolishness is just the opposite of that: the man or the woman who thinks only in terms of that which will bring him happiness as the central entity of his little world. That is foolishness, or folly.

What is the *house* referred to? This is the context of life. The woman dwells very near the center of that house and has a tremendous mission, a great task, and in its fulfillment, exceeding high and wondrous honors. If she fulfills this task, she builds the house. If she does not fulfill the task, she tears it down bit by bit, piece by piece until it lies a shambles at her feet or falls a wreck upon her head. Let us look at three things necessary to be considered in relation to our text.

The woman is a home builder in relation (1) to her husband, (2) to her children, and (3) to society 'round about her.

Our text does not say anything about the woman's husband, but the husband is the head of her house; he is, under Christ, the center of her life. The man takes the wife; the wife does not take the man. In the godly sense of this, the woman gives herself to her husband, and she becomes subject to him even as Christ becomes the head of the church and calls upon us who have been redeemed by Him to give ourselves subject to our heavenly bridegroom. So also the woman: in the marriage ceremony she vows that she will keep herself unto her husband as a woman in all the aspects of womanliness. She is building a home when her womanliness, her sexuality, is such that not only her husband knows and can safely trust in her but all the world knows—if they know her at all—that *there* is a woman who belongs to one man. She does not flaunt her womanliness in the eyes of men in a flirtatious manner or in any other way that would cast down the image that she is the faithful wife of one man in all that she is as a woman.

It is so important that we do not say *one* thing in our vows and *another* thing in our lives. It is so important when we have vowed to be faithful to Jesus Christ that in all of our lives before the world we show forth that faithfulness. If we vow faithfulness to Jesus Christ and do not show it forth, we live a lie. The woman lies who vows at the marriage altar faithfulness to her husband—to the degree that she exerts her power over other men even in a minor matter, even in an 'innocent,' flirtatious manner, even in the manner of her dress that she advertises to other men the peculiar relationships of her womanhood that belong only to her husband; to that extent, I say, she lives a lie. I say this because it must be said in days like these. I say it pleadingly, though I say it authoritatively, on the basis of the Word of God: she who regards this thing in wisdom builds her house; she who disregards this—no matter how outwardly faithful she may be —tears it down with her hands.

This is also true with regard to the support and encouragement she gives her husband. I know this because I am a husband: husbands are not the towers of strength they sometimes like their wives, their children, and the world to believe they are. Sometimes husbands just crack because of the awful pressures that come upon them in life. What does God give a man a help meet for? He gives him a help that is meet, that is suitable unto him, who, in the moment when he would falter, will encourage him and build him up and send him back to the battle, whatever the battle may be. He knows that back there in that little home of his is a woman who loves him and supports him and believes in him, who will stand by him even if all the world falls in upon him. That is the woman that builds her house. She who forsakes her husband in the moment of his weakness, in the moment of his trial, in the moment of his troubles does not build her house—she tears it down with her hands.

Yes, in this—and I am speaking to Christian wives now—they must pray *with* their husbands if they are Christian husbands; and if not, even more they must pray *for* them. There must be always this experience and this wisdom. And, believe me, talking about women, I believe in my ministerial experience I have seen more true wisdom in the women than in the men of these churches that I have ministered to. It is not the wisdom of decision, perhaps; but it is the wisdom of heart understanding, the wisdom that sees and without a word compensates for the weakness of others, the wisdom that remains silent and yet it is strong. I see this in many godly women, and I have seen more godliness in women than I have in men. They have a wisdom to see that the relationship with their husbands ripens through the years; and even as the physical becomes less and less the center of that relationship, the spiritual moves in and becomes greater and greater until there is that beautiful union and communion every day, every hour of the day and every day of the year that is like unto heaven; and, you know, the way that we get used to the idea of heaven is to get used to a little bit of it on the earth; home is where that heaven begins.

Then, finally, in the relationship to her husband there is labor—oh, what labor! In Proverbs 31 we read about the virtuous woman. I sometimes feel sorry for the wives when I read this. This is God's Word; and if they are to live up to that kind of activity, they must be stronger than men. Yet, just the same, there is a strength that is not in the body, that is not in the arm; and that is the strength of faithful and loyal support and labor—the labor of love that does not demand anything in return but that she may serve with her hands.

It is not the house. It is that family unit, that spiritual unity. The wife is married not only to the man but, in a sense, to his whole life; and she is so married to it that she is the one who will support it with the labor of her hands and with the love of her heart, with the constancy of her soul until she lays down the tools of her earthly warfare and enters into her heavenly reward. This is the way to build your house, wives. And I want to say, by way of interpretation, that those who are not yet wives must also look forward to this; this is the holy ideal God's Word lays down for you.

Second, in her relationship to her children, hers is the most important task; it has always been so. In her child's early years, it is her fingers that mold and shape that life. It is she who first must learn to walk that tight-rope of showing love and support and comfort to her babe and yet being strong enough and firm enough not to let that little bundle of life grow into a king or queen ruling that home by tantrum. It is she who must begin the work of discipline in the life of the child because she spends the most time with that child in the years that are really most formative in terms of personality, character, habits, and manner of life; and these habits and character are not basically changed even when the 'new birth' comes and changes the inner heart. Thus she builds her house.

If, on the other hand, she takes the center of the home; if she comes to her children and gets love from them because she needs that love (and perhaps in so doing rejects the love of her husband) and clutches to her bosom the love of her children, she destroys them and tears down the house that she is supposed to be building. She tears it down with her heart when she places her own needs (even the spiritual or psychological as well as the physical) in the middle of things and demands and demands and demands—sometimes very subtly, sometimes by charging her husband and children with ingratitude—but yet demands that everything keep coming *her* way. God made the godly woman to *give* and to *serve*—not to receive and treasure and cling and clutch things to herself.

With regard to her children, this is the time to teach them that a father is a father, that a father loves and that a father also expects obedience. I must refer to my own dear mother, who has since last Mother's Day gone to heaven. She taught me to love, to respect, and to honor my father. *He* did not teach me these things. He taught me to fear him; he taught me to obey him. But it was *she* who taught me that he loved me—and he did love me dearly. In those childhood days I could not see his love because of the sternness of his character; but my loving mother taught me to respect and to fear and to love my father. And never once in all my childhood days did my mother ever take my side or anybody's side against the man who was her husband, with whom she lived as a faithful wife for sixty-three years. Never once did she allow a wedge to be driven between her and him or between us and our father.

She must also teach her children to honor the faith insofar as she has these early, molding years under her charge. She must teach them about their Father which is in heaven. That old gospel song, which many of us who have gray hairs remember with a little bit of nostalgia, "My Mother's Prayers Have Followed Me," is true. It was my mother's prayers and my mother's life that first taught me a little bit of what God is like. I learned much more in my theological training, but the heart-education came at my mother's knee. In her own life I learned what prayer is, I learned what dependence is, I learned what submission is—because it was always my dear mother who went about calming and quieting us down, saying, "Let us not give place to wrath," when we were unjustly treated by others. It was my mother who spoke to my father in the same vein and in the same tone and kept his Irish temper from getting him into trouble. It was she who went about showing us what true submission to God in His Word, in His Commandments, and also in His Providence really means. Not only did she teach it to us, but she also lived it before us; and I thank God for this memory. What a terrible scandal the world would be without such mothers.

I do not want to give place to sentimentality, but that old saying is true: "The hand that rocks the cradle is the hand that rules the world." I am afraid that is the trouble with the world—the failure in part, at least, of motherhood. The hand that has rocked the cradle has ruled the world *badly* because of the sins that have produced an ungodly generation, the generation of which I am a part. By God's grace I was spared, and I plead with you mothers and mothers-to-be who still have something you can do in this matter: *save your children.* Save your children from contributing to the deliquency of the world in which we live. Show it not by trying to be equal and bold and independent as the world would have you to be; but show it by being true wives, true mothers, and true examples of godly living, tenderness, faithfulness, and submission.

A woman is not just a woman in her home and among her children. She is a woman when she goes out into the world. The woman in society has an aura, a kind of radiance—or a counterfeit of it. It is that aura which I would consider in the third place. Proverbs 31:31 says, ". . . her own works praise her in the gates." The gate was the street in the middle of the city. She had to go out into the world; and the people said, 'That is a woman, indeed! Look at what she has done! Look at her family! Look at her husband!' They honor her, and "Her children arise up, and call her blessed; her husband also, and he praiseth her. Many daughters have done virtuously, but thou excellest them all." Because of the kind of woman she was, the kind of aura she had about her, her husband felt that there was no other woman like her in the world. That is the way every husband ought to feel toward his wife—even if she only *begins* to be worthy according to this pattern.

What is this aura? We have it in I Peter 3:4, "But let it be the hidden man of the heart, in that which is not corruptible, even the ornament of a meek and quiet spirit, which is in the sight of God of great price." Now, ladies, I know this is hard, very hard, because you are sinners. We men are sinners, too. Meekness is laid upon the human race—that is, all who would be called 'godly' by Jesus in the Beatitudes; but meekness and the quiet spirit, particularly, is the quality that you must seek. You see, do you not, that this is a big order for you? It is an attitude which you need in your home and among your children; you need it in your heart, and it is planted there by the working of the Spirit with the Word of God through such sermons as this; and when it gets down into your heart, it will come out in a radiance of beauty and a glow that not all the beauticians of this wide world can produce. It is that inner beauty of meekness and quietness.

Again, Proverbs 31 says of the virtuous woman, ". . . in her tongue is the law of kindness." Is that true of you? And you girls, who do not yet have husbands? Or is your tongue a deadly poison, full of evil, leading astray, setting afire the whole course of nature?

The woman must fulfill her role in the world. God made you women, and he made most women that each might be the wife of one husband. That is God's natural role for her. This is what most young women will finally become.

God has some things for unmarried women to do. I want to say something about that, and I hope you will see this as a gem of wisdom not from me but from God Himself. Even the unmarried woman is given her womanliness to be a support; she is always to be a satellite, never a sun in her own right. We have many examples of this. Anna, who was in the temple, a widow of four score years. What did she do there? She prayed; and because she prayed, God honored her by one of the very first sights of the face of His incarnate Son. What a ministry! Again, we have Dorcas, another widow. She made clothes for the needy; her hands were busy all the time; and when she died, they brought them out to remember in love. She was a satellite. If the woman who is unmarried, or a widow, wants to serve as a woman, she can be a servant of Jesus Christ either directly or indirectly in the church or for somebody in this world who needs her; and she is happiest when she is fulfilling a need because that is the way God made her. When she begins to concentrate upon herself, upon her comfort, then happiness flies out the window and does not come back until she returns to her first work.

Now, in conclusion, I want to say to all of the ladies here this morning, You are the daughters of Eve, and that is the trouble with you. Remember what 'your mother' did: she reversed the course of nature. She was supposed to follow her husband, but she did not follow her husband. She led him, and she led him into sin. She was first in sin, Paul tells us; and God visited her with a curse—with very great difficulty in child-bearing so that child-bearing was like death to her in those early years *because* she was the first in sin. But even in this humble and somewhat humiliating role God promised to save her if she would submit to Him faithfully. This is the problem, ladies, you are the daughters of Eve! Of course, you men are the sons of Adam; and his weakness was just as contemptible in God's sight as the over-assertiveness of Eve in the matter of the temptation.

But there is another one of whom you might be daughters. You might be daughters of Sara, the humble, submissive wife of Abraham, who even when she was not doing things exactly right, nevertheless, showed that she was submissive to her husband and called him "lord: whose daughters ye are, as long as ye do well, and are not afraid with any amazement" (I Peter 3:6). Which means if you fulfill your godly role in your home, where God has called you, out of the fear of God and love to the Lord Jesus and a desire to build your house rather than tear it down with your hands, then, indeed, if you seek to do this, God will bless you and give you a crown that in honor and glory and beauty is a crown no queen on earth could ever touch or claim.

I talked to a group of ladies in another city recently and taught them these very things from I Peter 3:1-6. One of them afterward spoke to me and said, "You know, Pastor, when you talked to us this way, it made us proud that we are women. It made us feel as if we would not give up our place in life for all the wealth of the world." And that is the way, under Christ, that I would have you feel this morning. If this is a message for Mother's Day, you may accept it as such. If not, at least it is out of God's Word, and it is the burden of my heart this morning.

FATHER IN HEAVEN, we ask Thy blessing upon these words. We do beseech Thee, O Lord, that insofar as they have been spoken in truth and in verity, so write them upon the tables of our hearts that we may never forget them. We pray that what is not of God in this message may be obliterated forever from our minds that the Lord Jesus Christ may have all honor and praise in all that we have said. God, bless our homes. God, bless our mothers—the mothers that are and the mothers that are yet to be. And, God, through them bless the church and the nation for Jesus' sake. Amen.

May 11, 1969

Lawrence R. Eyres

A HERITAGE FOR OUR COVENANT CHILDREN

Psalm 78:1-8

This Psalm was written by Asaph and closely associated with David's time for the purpose of urging upon the parents of Israel the heritage that they had from the days of their first becoming a nation, with the hope that the parents would seek the Lord and teach the same to following generations. The duty to teach Israel's heritage unto their children is particularly enforced by the history of Israel's constant and persistent apostasy. This apostasy is epitomized in the rebel spirit of Ephraim, which later (after the death of Solomon) erupted into schism in Israel, severing the ten tribes from Judah and Benjamin.

The Psalm begins in a fatherly tone, urging close attention. The Psalmist declares his intention to teach some of the deeper, subtler truths of the past. Therefore, what follows is much more than a chronicle of Israel's history from the Exodus to the establishing of David's kingdom. It is a lesson in contrasts: God's mighty deliverances contrasted with the rebellion of Israel, followed by judgments, which in turn are followed by superficial repentances, followed again by God's indulgent lifting of His judgments. This circle would inevitably lead to a new circle of apostasy, judgment, repentance, deliverance. Now, the source of this unpurged wickedness is traced to the spirit of Ephraim which led that tribe to seek preeminence. As a matter of fact, he had the preeminence from the days of Joshua, especially in the days of the Judges. The tabernacle was in Shiloh in Ephraim; and it was at the end of this period that, due to this spirit of Ephraim, the Ark of the Covenant fell to the Philistines. As a judgment against Ephraim, God gave the Ark to Judah and, in due time, established David upon the throne of Israel.

If Israel had learned the lesson of Psalm 78, there would have been no division of the kingdom in the days of Rehoboam. But it was this still virulent spirit of Ephraim that wrought the disruption under

Jeroboam, an Ephraimite. It would seem that the dictum of the philosopher Hegel was true then as now: all that man learns from history is that man never learns anything from history!

Coming now to the text before us, especially in verses 3 to 8, the inspired Psalmist lays upon the heads of the families of Israel that they must teach these sobering lessons to their children after them. And, most interestingly, in verse 4 we read, "We will not hide them [these sober truths] from *their* children." We might have expected the Psalmist to say, 'our children.' In a sense this would have been true; but, in terms of the covenant, their children were the children of their godly ancestors, who had a just claim upon their young and impressionable hearts. They belonged to the godly forbears of Israel because Israel belonged to the God of Abraham, of Isaac, and of Jacob. This is no less true today. Our children are *covenant children.* It was just that that made Amram and Jochebed defy the decree of Pharaoh regarding the baby Moses. It was not so much that they refused to acknowledge Pharaoh's right over their child, but that Moses was God's covenant entrustment to them, and it was not within their own power to violate that trust and give what was not theirs to Pharaoh! To put it differently, our children belong to the past that they might march into the future in the continuation of God's covenant people throughout the history of the world. The spirit of Ephraim would break the connection. We must resist that spirit with all that is in us, under the blessing of God.

Our children are God's gift to us. If we are Christians, they are God's; and it is our responsibility to hide them in Christ. It is our responsibility to say 'No' to the world, which in every subtle way would put its stamp upon their minds and hearts. Our children are given us to raise for God. They are not given to us for our own comfort, our joy—although we get comfort and joy from them; but they are given to us by God to raise for Him. God has set fathers and, under them, mothers to rule over their own families well, having their "children in subjection with all gravity," with all godliness.

God did miracle after miracle to keep the three million people of the Hebrew nation alive where there was no natural means of life whatsoever. Yet in spite of this there was apostasy in Israel.

> They kept not the covenant of God, and refused to walk in his law; And forgat his works, and his wonders that he had shewed them.
>
> . . . And they tempted God in their heart by asking meat for their lust. Yea, they spake against God; they said, Can God furnish a table in the wilderness? (Psalm 78:10, 11, 18, 19).
>
> Now all these things happened unto them for ensamples: and they are written for our admonition, upon whom the ends of the world are come (I Corinthians 10:11).
>
> And thou shalt teach them diligently unto thy children, and shalt talk of them when thou sittest in thine house, and when thou walkest by the way, and when thou liest down, and when thou risest up (Deuteronomy 6:7).

This lesson from Deuteronomy is a lesson for us today. We must regard our children as being the children that God has given us.

> We will not hide them from their children, shewing to the generation to come the praises of the Lord, and his strength, and his wonderful works that he hath done (Psalm 78:4).

These children are the children of a generation gone before, a generation with a godly heritage; and so the Psalmist tells us our duty is: to bring our children into the line of the godly heritage of our spiritual ancestors. We must fill their minds and their hearts with the facts of the heritage to which they belong.

Why is it that young people from so-called Christian homes are not out on university campuses opposing everything that is raging against the knowledge of God, against God-given authority? Is it possibly because we have not taught them

> Let every soul be subject unto the higher powers. For there is no power but of God: the powers that be are ordained of God? (Romans 13:1).

Is it possibly because we have not told them that all rightful and lawful authority is an extension of the scepter and crown of King Jesus and that to be obedient to rightful authority is to be obedient to Jesus Christ, who is the only absolute King of our lives?

Failure to do this is the failure of the home and the church jointly. The unit of the church is the family. It is a task of massive inculcation, or inundation, of the things of God into the hearts of our children.

How much time do you spend *talking* to your children about the things of God? How much time do you spend *telling* your children the meaning of today's world happenings in the light of the Word of God? How much time do you spend *warning* your children of the danger of rebellion—not only that it will bring trouble to them in this life, but also that it will bring them up against the wrath of God in the life to come? How much time do you spend *praying* that God will change the hearts of your children and bring them to a saving faith in Jesus Christ? How much time do you spend *teaching* them the deep things of the Word of God? How much time do you spend *pleading* with them to give their hearts to the Lord Jesus? This is not easy.

It is your duty to take the Word of God, the things of God, and the history of God's people and to make your children *feel* them. It is to make your children feel that they are marching at the head of a great army of saints whose columns stretch back through the centuries to the Reformation, to the times of the Apostles, to the days of the Lord Jesus Christ, even to the days of the children of Israel as they passed out of Egypt and marched through the wilderness. We must teach our children that they belong to that great heritage.

We must teach them that they do not belong to this secular world. We have to teach our children that they must resist the infiltrating thoughts of this secular world in order that they might know and live as those who belong to the mighty army of saints of God in the past, which continues unto this very day and will continue to march across the pages of history till the Lord Jesus Christ comes again on the clouds of heaven.

Only you can do it because God has raised you up as parents to do it. We help you, but I have not the least sympathy with the Christian parent who gives his children to the Sunday school and says, "I'll bring him. I'll come and get him. You educate him for Christ." If the Sunday school is not regarded as a supplement of what you teach them in the home, the Sunday school is not going to work—unless God is marvelously merciful beyond His promises.

It has to be the church and the home together as a mighty combine of education, of teaching, of inculcation, of example, of prayer—everything that goes to make the hearts of His children right. And *until we do this,* we are not going to see any great change in the terrible trends of the day in which we live.

To give you some idea of the content of that teaching of heritage, *first,* it means that we must connect our children with that living legend of the church in ages gone by. How much do *you* know about church history? It is time, dear friends, that we learn about the great history of the Christian church. We have been talking about the Reformation, the Reformers, the Puritans, and our godly ancestors. In this church the last two or three years we have been making available to you, at the lowest prices possible, great books written for the common people by the Puritans and others since then that you might know the history of the church, that you might know what God has done in ages past, that you and your children might identify with the church in ages past. Be sure you use these sources.

Second, it means that we must teach our children the nature of God, the great God of wonders, doing mighty deeds for His own people and for their salvation.

Third, we must also teach them their own nature, the fact that they are hell-deserving sinners and that all of them have the spirit of Ephraim in them that seeks to have the preeminence and does not want to submit humbly to the leadership of God, His Word, and His servants. We must teach them their own total depravity.

Fourth, we must teach them not to trust in their own wisdom and not to trust in their own hearts.

Finally, we must teach them to hope in the Covenant Redeemer of Israel:

> That they might set their hope in God, and not forget the works of God, but keep his commandments (Psalm 78:7).

Until they know who God is; until they know that they should be identified with the great army of the faithful in the past; until they know what terrible sinners they are; until they know the Gospel in all of its beautiful contrasts; until they know that God alone is the One in whom they can put their absolute and everlasting hope—these children of ours are not going to be saved, and we are going to fail in our duty as Christian parents.

I propose to you a sort of violent upheaval in our family lives to take hold of that family structure, overhaul it, and cast out the idols, whatever they may be. An idol, you know, is anything that teaches what is contrary to the Word of God. Cast it out. Until *you* take over the control, the rule, and the running of your home in a full and formal way, you are never going to get anywhere in this matter of teaching your children the right ways of the Lord.

I propose this to you: *the only sure alternative* to finding that in the last day your sons and daughters are doomed to suffer the vengeance of eternal fire *is to raise them in the manner that I have suggested*: raise them as a continuation of the stream of the godly in the past ages of history; raise them as those who *know* that they belong to the Covenant God; raise them as those who are willing to fight and resist all efforts of the world to win them into its camp.

If you do not want to see your children perish in eternal flames—and I mean exactly that—then you are going to have to do what the Psalmist commands, to say

> We will not hide these things from our children, shewing to the generation to come the praises of the Lord, and his strength, and his wonderful works that he hath done. For he established a testimony in Jacob, and appointed a law in Israel, which he commanded our fathers, that they should make them known to their children: That the generation to come might know them, even the children which should be born; who should arise and declare them to their children. That they might set their hope in God, and not forget the works of God, but keep his commandments (Psalm 78:4-7).

FATHER, we ask Thee now that Thou wilt take these words and write them upon our hearts, these truths, O Lord, and make them the very warp and woof of our thinking. God, forgive us that we have offered our sons and daughters to the worldly Molochs of today, allowing them to pass through fires of influence which win and woo them away from the God of heaven.

God, help us to see that this is a battle to the death, not only for us and our children, but for the whole church of God. Indeed, conflicts are rising sharper and sharper in our day. Lord, may we be willing to cast our all in with Jesus and His thoughts and His church and His cause, and His covenant. For His name's sake, we ask it. Amen.

February 15, 1969

Joel H. Nederhood

THE GLORY OF GOD IN CREATION

Genesis 1:26, 27

I want to talk about the impact of the doctrine of evolution in our present world and reflect with you on our reaction as Christian people to this very devastating view of man. Frequently we as Christian people who are committed to the creationist view of origins tend to write off evolution as a doctrine which some people hold to be true but which we know not to be true and which we, consequently, feel is of little effect in our world. In fact, I think this is one of our great problems as Christians: we frequently analyze the opinions and positions of the opposition, demolish them with our philosophies and doctrines, and then act as if they no longer exist. But I would like to remind all of you that God's people today are called to be His people in a world which is dominated everywhere by the evolutionary view of man.

We are frequently disturbed today by the many crises which confront us. Perhaps none is more disturbing than that found on the campuses of our land. The revolutions occurring there, our feeling that the younger generation is rapidly slipping away from us—all this is a part of the fact that we are living in an age in which man has lost his bearings not only concerning God but concerning himself. Who man is, what he is, and what he is here for has been completely forgotten.

It is interesting that at the end of the nineteenth century men began to speak of a *deus abscondicus*, a hidden God; and as they spoke about the hiddenness of God, it was not very long before they began to speak of an *anthropos abscondicus,* a hidden man, a man for whom it is no longer possible to discover the nature of his being and purpose for existence. Today we find the logical conclusion to both these events in the history of human thought. The hidden God has given way to a "dead" God, and we are gazing upon a civilization which is in shambles because man has begun to feel that, in a sense, he, too, is dead. Man is not dead in the sense that he does not possess life, but he is coming to the awful conclusion that he is dead so far as a glorious future is concerned—that he is nothing more than a mass of protoplasm here for a short time and then wiped away, a clod among all the other clods in the world.

This is the crisis of our age: man has come to believe that he is nothing more than a part of nature. Anybody who is anybody believes this. Most of those in positions of intellectual responsibility are continually pushing the idea that man is a part of nature. *The American Scholar* is replete with articles by men of stature, who are giving leadership to our country and the world, who are saying that the evolutionary principles of Charles Darwin, however imperfect they may be from the viewpoint of the science of genetics, have been proved to be the essential insights man needs and must use in determining who he is and what his future is. This is the dominant position in this country and in our world.

We have not seen anything yet so far as crisis in our land is concerned, but the future is unutterably grim—not because we have enemies across the sea, but because our nation has capitulated to a naturalistic view of human history and human nature. This is why it is so important that people who stand within the Christian tradition, and the Reformed position specifically, understand what is happening and learn the structure and the dimensions of their responsibility. The evolutionary point of view is making itself felt on a variety of levels. I will mention just three of them so that we may together be impressed with the scope of the problem confronting us.

The evolutionary concept, most importantly, is making itself felt within the sphere of education in the United States. James Conant, former president of Harvard University and ambassador to Germany, a formative mind, particularly in connection with junior high school education, in a recent article, "Man Thinking about Man," has written, "In the years ahead we will discover the implications of the fact that man is a part of nature." That insight is already dominating the structure of American education. As citizens we should be aware of what is going on in public education: our schools, our teachers colleges, and our students are being programmed hour after hour, day after day to believe that one can study about this world and about history and social relationships without any reference to the Lordship of Jesus and the creative power of God.

We should not be overly disturbed that prayers and Bible reading have been removed from schools so long as it is against the law to say, "God made our world and He still rules it now through Jesus Christ." Millions and millions and millions of our children have been subjected to that kind of education. Some of us here tonight are interested in Christian education. Let us remember that Christian education is not really an option in the United States; in thousands of communities the only education available is one that denies the creatorship of God.

Another area in which the creatorship of God is being denied is in the laws of our land. There is no longer a description of law and punishment for misdemeanors and felonies in terms of a higher rule of God over all of life which all men must obey. Law is now seen as an expression of what the majority feels to be right or wrong at a given time. You have seen that happen in your State in connection with the liberalization of abortion laws. Some time ago I had an opportunity to participate in hearings on this subject in the State of Illinois. I listened to witness after witness say that human life in the prenatal state could be disposed of at the whim of the mother and anyone else who had a particular stake in the development of that innocent, unborn child. There was complete disregard for the fact that such an organism is already in the hand of God and represents a potential human being. It was frightening to sit there during those hours and hear educated, genteel people, who probably even wanted to be known as Christian, speak about killing in such a calloused way.

Another area of life today in which we have an opportunity to observe the corruption which results from evolutionary thought is the new pornography being produced at a sickening rate. *Portnoy's Complaint,* by Philip Roth, is an example. This young writer, supposedly a man of great sensitivity and literary ability, has written a book which 20 years ago would have been circulated on typewritten pages in a barracks. This new pornography flooding the market and enjoying critical acclaim is an expression of the devolution which comes at the end of evolution, when man has finally come to the conclusion that he is little more than an animal.

I am indebted to Francis Schaeffer of L'Abri, Switzerland, for a very useful analysis of modern pornography. He says this pornography demonstrates that men who have abandoned hope of finding anything worthwhile in life on other levels are in desperation probing the limits of their sexuality on the chance that there they may discover meaning and importance. These are not just ordinary dirty books produced to give people a thrill for a moment or two. Rather, they are an expression of the depths of our modern predicament in which men long schooled to think of themselves as nothing more than a part of nature are now demonstrating to themselves that this is so. Thus they flounder in the cesspool of their own iniquity, fulfilling in their lives the prophecy of God in Romans 1:18-21, which tells us that God finally delivers men over to their own vile passions. Men are expressing this before our very eyes. The philosophy that "man is simply a part of nature" finally leads down into the sub-basement of human consciousness, where men grovel about in the desperate hope that there within the gloom they will discover something which will make life meaningful and worth while.

We are living in a cultural crisis of inestimable proportions as this paralyzing falsehood persuades men, "You are just a part of nature, here today and gone tomorrow." Our land is in the grip of that falsehood. I would like to reiterate that all of our educational structure in the United States is programming our young people to come to that conclusion. I say this, realizing that many wonderful, God-fearing people are working hard to make something fine and useful out of public education. But right now we are talking about the big picture in the United States, and the big picture is very grim indeed: our nation is in pursuit of the false ideology that man is the product of an evolutionary process. From now on everything—newspapers, magazines, books, schools, television, radio, movies—is going to be programmed to make us believe that falsehood.

What must be our reaction to this? We can talk about these things yet feel as if they are happening outside us; but this culture is impinging upon us, too; and our faith sometimes begins to shake a little with everything else that is shaking. We have to reaffirm within our fellowship that we have another message, an insight from the Word of God. We must ask God to burn our message into our hearts again because complacency is our problem. *We must bring our message to the world.*

It is encouraging to remember that as the holy Scriptures give us knowledge of God, at the very same instant they give us knowledge of ourselves as well. John Calvin saw this and discussed the fascinating problem of how we are going to learn about God: Is it not necessary first to understand ourselves? Calvin came to the conclusion that, as part of God's grace, knowledge of oneself as a man and knowledge of God as one's Creator are joined together (*Institutes,* Book I, Chapter 1). We rejoice this evening that while we sing praises to God, read His Word, and learn about Him and about Jesus Christ, we discover who we are and who our fellow men are.

What is the message the Bible brings that rescues us from the hopelessness and bleakness of the naturalistic point of view, which pervades our world? The message of Genesis 1:26, 27 is that we are the image bearers of the living God. This is the mystery of our personality. It means that before the Fall man possessed certain qualities which were holy; he was righteous then and possessed a knowledge of God that was glorious. But there is more to the image of God than simply those attributes of man's being which existed before the Fall and were destroyed by it: his capability of imagination, of laughter and of weeping, his capability of living in communion with others, his capability of exercising himself creatively in terms of certain goals, and, particularly, his glorious privilege of entering into the covenant relationship with the God of heaven and earth are all part of God's image in man. This is part of the knowledge that makes us rejoice. When we are saved we understand that we are not simply part of a process which will terminate in the dust of the grave, but that God has laid His finger upon us for time and eternity, and we will live forever in His presence.

Man is the image bearer of God in his soul and also in his body, which can become the temple of the Holy Spirit (I Corinthians 6:19).

This is the message that we have to proclaim in this world. Whenever we hear messages that claim that men are simply a part of nature, we must say vehemently, "That is a lie! Man has been created in the image of the living God." And God calls us to demonstrate that knowledge and that understanding in everything we do.

I believe personally that this is one of the things that make it so necessary for Christians to erect their own institutions of learning, not just so they can have prayer in them but in order to show the young people entrusted to our covenant homes that they are the image bearers of the living God. And that has something to say about everything they study. History, sociology, economics, science, the arts, literature, agriculture, commerce—each takes on a different cast when one believes that man is the image bearer of the living God.

We have another calling in response to this great insight God has entrusted to our care. Those who understand that man is the image bearer of the living God should be on the forefront of every activity to bring relief to the suffering and starving, to bring justice among the peoples of the world. I am thinking particularly of the race problem in this country, which during the 50's and 60's has been dominated by people of liberal theological orientation. Today we see that their solutions have not actually done anybody any good. But we who understand that men are the image bearers of God—where have we been in this great crisis?

Before leaving the office I received a letter from a teacher, a Negro. She and her Christian colleagues in the public schools of Harlem are organizing to bring a witness to the Lord Jesus Christ. She said, "I know, of course, that many of you who are evangelicals have not always stood with us who are trying to bring the name of Christ into the situation, and frequently evangelical communities have been guilty of fortifying prejudice and even guilty of furthering hatred." Maybe I am particularly bitter on this subject. Forgive me if I am. But it is always so disconcerting whenever I deal with this subject over the air to receive the bitterest letters of all from people who claim to understand that men have been created in the image of the living God. There is no place for prejudice of any kind in our congregations. We must be in the forefront of every cause designed to bring about racial justice in our country.

Many who stand outside the Christian tradition are disturbed by today's trends—by the new pornography, for example; but they are not proclaiming the message that is needed: We are confronted by all these deformations of human nature because man is a sinner and must, therefore, respond to his predicament by repenting of his sin and turning to the living God. It will *not* do for us simply to say, "Look what's happening to our world. It's going to destruction! Let's separate ourselves from it and let it go!" God calls us as His people, who believe His Word is truth to proclaim to all men: "Repent, for the day of the Lord is at hand." This is the message which we must raise with increased fervency because we understand that what we are seeing is not due to the reality that men are not yet perfect but is the result of the fact that when we were still untainted by sin, by our free will we chose to live in rebellion against the living God, and therefore all men live beneath the curse. Repent of your sin! This is the message that the Christian church must raise today as never before.

If there is any one who feels depressed because of the direction things are taking in our world—or the way things are going in your own life—God comes to you tonight and says, "Believe." The reason your life is frequently disappointing is not because you have not yet reached a higher stage of evolutionary development but because you are living beneath the curse of God's wrath. You are a sinner and God is calling you not simply to weep tears over disappointments but to repent of your sins, to confess as the prodigal son did when he came back, "I have sinned against heaven itself." That is the message to men today, a message which goes back to the opening verses of the great Book of Books, which lies open before us tonight. We are image bearers of the living God, but in our natural state we are image bearers who are living in rebellion. We must turn from our sin, and we must confront the world with that great call to repentance and conversion.

The book of Jonah speaks to people like us. We are very thankful that we are not a part of the world which is going to destruction; but sometimes we can be afraid to preach the gospel of repentance because we know that our God is a merciful God, who sometimes brings salvation and repentance into the lives of people with whom we prefer not to associate—even into the lives of our enemies. Nevertheless, we must bring the message that man has fallen and must turn from his sin.

We must also proclaim with joy that *the image of God in man can be restored through faith in Jesus Christ our Lord.* This is the glorious message of the gospel that must be hurled across our country from every church in which people rejoice together because they know the Lord Jesus Christ is the One in whom it is possible for men to be restored. Colossians 3:9, 10 talks about this, "Lie not one to another, seeing that ye have put off the old man with his deeds and have put on the new man which is renewed in knowledge after the image of him that created him." Jesus is the One who is Prophet, Priest, and King, fulfilling His great work of redemption through the obedience which He worked through His perfect life; and on the cross of Calvary He made new what Adam had destroyed. As in Adam all men have been lost, in Christ there is the possibility of renewal of the image of God.

Hebrews 1:3 describes Jesus as the One who is the image bearer of God *par excellence.* Jesus appears on the pages of human history as the One who represents God in all of His fullness. If it were not for Jesus, who is the One through whom God has created all things, who is the One in whom are hid all the treasures of wisdom and knowledge (Colossians 2:3), there would be no hope at all. When we sinful men turn to Him, we will be transformed and life will be important; there will be new hope, new goals, and new meaning. This is what we have to see personally. This is why Jesus is important to me. If it were not for Jesus, there would be no use preaching, no use praying, no use singing. *If* Jesus be not true, then the world *is* just an evolutionary process hurtling on to some unknown and unimaginable goal, a process which some day shall be terminated when our universe shall explode in some cataclysmic fury or implode as energy turns in upon itself.

I suggest to you tonight that the only way we and our children can keep our balance as this world rushes down the awful path it has chosen is by focusing our attention as never before upon Jesus, remembering that in this Person, and specifically at Calvary's cross, an answer to all human questions was finally formulated by God Himself. At Calvary all the mystery, the contradiction, and irrationality of human existence was resolved when God poured out His wrath upon His only begotten Son, the Son of His love. We have to look at that Jesus. We have to remember that without Him there is no hope at all. We must placard this Jesus before the world as Paul did when he brought Him to the Galatians. The cross is the only place where there is possibility of salvation. Those who look at Jesus experience the renewal of the image of God within their lives; they put on a new man, a new man which is being formed in righteousness and holiness and which is being prepared for that interminable eternity when we will be forever before the face of our Creator and Redeemer, our beautiful Savior, the King of creation.

And so our world hurtles along tonight, and we know not where it is going. We only know our duty is to bring Jesus to it incessantly and with persistence, knowing that God in His great grace will bring to the foot of the cross those people whom He has known from all eternity; and in those people the restored image of God will be revealed.

What about you? Do you know that Jesus? Do you know that there is no hope outside of Him—none at all? The only place where a man should dare to stand today is at the foot of Calvary, washed in Jesus' blood. That is where you must stand tonight. As you stand there, you will not succumb to this awful world view that encroaches on every side. And if you stand there, God will use you to withstand the awful forces of this age.

Help us to feel, heavenly Father, the serious quality of the times in which we are living now. Grant that we may embrace once more tonight with fervent love this wonderful message which gives us a new direction and a new understanding of ourselves and of our world. We thank Thee that we may know that we are not the product of some impersonal process, but that we have come into this world from Thy fingers, created in Thy image. Help us now in Jesus Christ to live as image bearers of the Almighty and use us in spite of the fact that we are dust and ashes. Use us somehow to make an impact upon this world which has chosen against Thee. Through Christ, we pray. Amen.

March 18, 1969